T0034517

Pedro's Yo-Yos

To my mother, and in memory of my father,
to whom I both owe my heritage —R. P.

For Jun's godparents—Abe Ignacio and Christine Araneta, for Michael and
Hwacha Kim, and for Ezekiel Bantulan Ebalaroza
Special thanks to Rick Brough, Jo Radovan, Jerome Cheng, and my wife, Holly
Kim, for their support during this project. —C. A.

Photos provided courtesy of the Flores family

Text copyright © 2024 by Roberto Peñas
Illustrations copyright © 2024 by Carl Angel

All rights reserved. No part of this book may be reproduced, transmitted, or stored in an information retrieval system in any form or by any means, electronic, mechanical, photocopying, recording, or otherwise, without written permission from the publisher.

LEE & LOW BOOKS INC., 95 Madison Avenue, New York, NY 10016
leeandlow.com

Edited by Cheryl Klein and Adam Rau
Book design by Maria Mercado
Book production by The Kids at Our House
The text is set in Neutraface.
The art was created digitally.

Manufactured in China by RR Donnelley
10 9 8 7 6 5 4 3 2 1
First Edition

Cataloging-in-Publication Data at Library of Congress
ISBN: 9781620145746 (HC) ISBN: 9781620149805 (EBK)

Pedro's Yo-Yos

How a Filipino Immigrant Came to America and Changed the World of Toys

by
Rob Peñas

illustrated by
Carl Angel

LEE & LOW BOOKS INC.
New York

Make it **flip, leap,** and **swing**.

Roll it down between your hands . . .

. . . or **spin it forward** on one leg.

The tricks you can do with it are nearly **endless**.

No wonder the yo-yo is one of the most successful toys ever made!

FLORES

And its popularity began with a Filipino immigrant seeking a better life abroad.

When Pedro Flores was born in 1896, Spain ruled over his country, the Philippines. The Spaniards forced their subjects to labor in the rice and abaca fields and refused to let them travel outside their villages without permission. Yoked under this harsh rule, many Filipinos longed to gain freedom over their own lives.

In their free time after school, Pedro and his friends played with a grooved disc carved from a water buffalo's horn. This simple toy was called a "yo-yo," which means "come back" in Tagalog, one of the many languages spoken in the Philippine Islands.

The boys had endless fun with the yo-yo, swinging it on a string and competing with each other to conjure up the fanciest moves.

The Philippine people rebelled against their colonial rulers,
right as Spain went to war against the United States. To escape this
situation, the Spanish sold the country to the Americans for
twenty million dollars—about three dollars per Filipino.

Pedro watched soldiers march through town, swaggering with confidence.
Officials followed, telling Filipinos they must now read and speak English.
Listening to his new teacher, Pedro learned about the United States,
a country across the vast ocean.

American engineers built a highway through Pedro's province, stretching farther than anyone could see. Then one by one, by foot and by cart, Filipinos did something they could not do before. They began to leave.

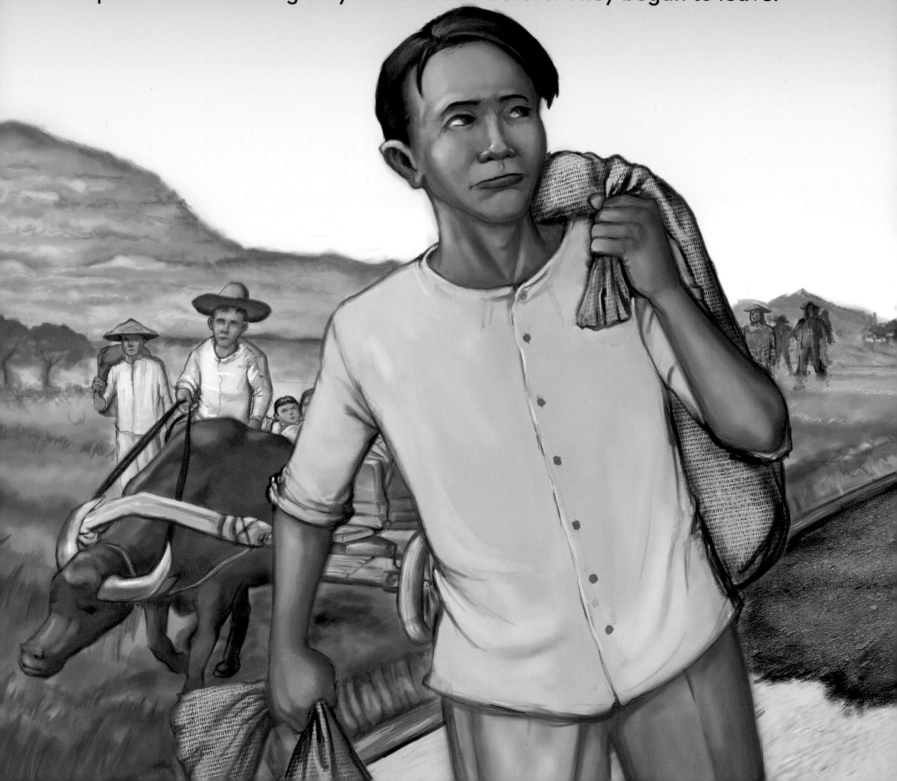

Letters came back, bringing hope for those who were weary and poor. In the United States, the letters said, people could live as they pleased. Why should Pedro miss a chance to create his own dream? When he was fifteen years old, he left for America too.

Pedro's ship passed through Hong Kong, where he marveled at its beautiful harbor at night, to the modern battle fleet in Yokohama, Japan. After a month at sea, where he became terribly seasick, his steamer docked in Honolulu.

Like his fellow kabayan, Pedro labored in the pineapple fields, under a burning sun, enduring long days with low pay. This was not why Pedro had come. After working for two years, Pedro journeyed to San Francisco, a city teeming with wooden houses, steep hills, and people of all races.

Pedro did not stay long. He spent years working on steamships bound for Mexico and Central America. One year he traveled to Guam. Another voyage took him to Alaska, where the vessel got stuck in ice. With no fresh water, the crew melted the ice to drink. And Pedro continued to become seasick often.

Eventually Pedro decided to further his education. He spoke English well, thanks to his teachers in the Philippines and his years of travel. Although he was eight years older than most of his classmates, he became one of the few students at that time to attend high school.

After a short time in college, Pedro moved to Santa Barbara, California, where he worked as a hotel bellhop, carrying people's suitcases up and down the stairs. Sometimes guests gave him a few coins; other times they gave him nothing. By now he was over thirty years old and felt no better off than when he left the Philippines. He wanted to find a way to work for himself.

Pedro stayed with a family whose little boy, too young for baseball, had a rubber ball and only Pedro to play with. Back and forth they tossed the ball for hours on end. Pedro knew he could make a much better toy.

Pedro carved two disks out of wood and a small axle to join them.

Then he twisted twine into a string to create a loop around the axle.

When he threw the yo-yo, the loop allowed it to spin or "sleep" at the end of the string before it rolled back up to his hand.

Pedro made it hop along the floor and spun it around his head in ever-larger circles. His eyes lit up. What other fantastic tricks could his yo-yo do?

Pedro taught the boy how to use this new toy . . . then the father . . . then the mother, then their aunties and neighbors. He carved eight to ten yo-yos a day, painting some with beautiful designs.

His yo-yos sold out in no time.

With the help of the boy's father, Pedro opened a factory to manufacture his yo-yos, but it couldn't keep up with demand. Investors helped him open a second and then a third factory. That still wasn't enough.

Soon, Pedro's factories were making hundreds of thousands of yo-yos a day. Other companies sold imitations called "twirlers" or "whirl-a-gigs." Pedro's advertisements simply proclaimed, "If it isn't a Flores, it isn't a yo-yo."

News spread quickly about this marvel called the "The Wonder Toy." Pedro came up with more tricks to show what the yo-yo could do—clever moves that became known as "Rock the Baby" . . .

"Loop the Loop" . . .

. . . and "Walk the Dog."

Pedro realized that when people saw the yo-yo in action, they clamored to get one for themselves. He hired kabayan to perform tricks outside candy stores and on street corners—anywhere children gathered. Boys and girls crowded around them wherever they went.

With his team of Filipino experts, Pedro toured cities nationwide, holding yo-yo competitions in movie theaters and other venues. Some contests rewarded those who could perform complicated tricks without making a mistake. Others challenged competitors to make their yo-yos spin at the string's end for the longest time. No one had ever promoted a toy this way before! A yo-yo craze swept across the land.

A Chicago businessman named Donald Duncan was impressed. The yo-yo sure was a darn good toy! Duncan offered to buy the company. He asked Pedro and his kabayan to stay on to promote the yo-yo throughout the country.

Pedro readily agreed. He now had the freedom to do anything he pleased, and he wanted to spend his time bringing enjoyment to children.

As years passed, the yo-yo grew in popularity. The word "yo-yo" became part of the English-language dictionary. In 1985, the crew on the NASA space shuttle *Discovery* showed one off in outer space, where the lack of gravity made it move really slooooowwwwwly while spinning really fast.

Yo-yo competitions are still held around the world,
with contestants of all ages creating amazing new tricks.

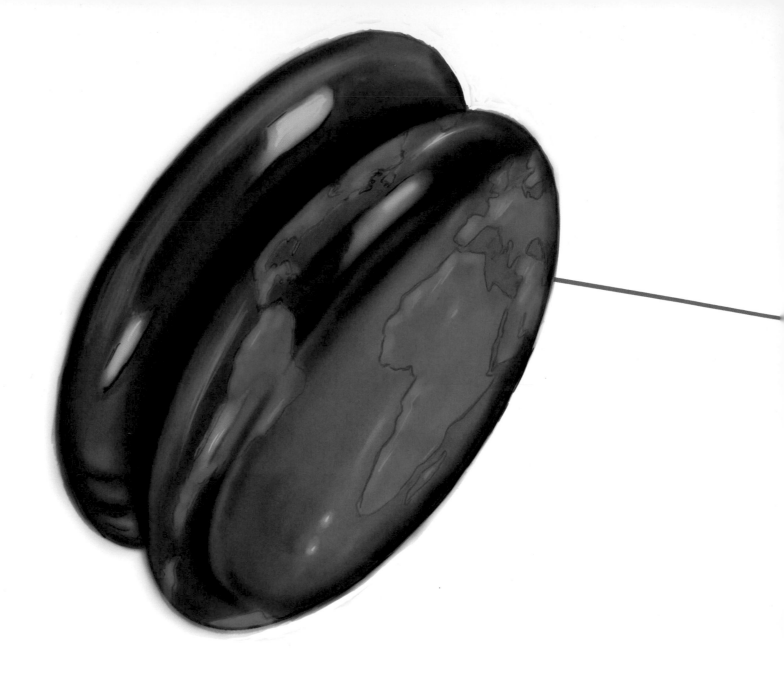

Pedro Flores didn't invent the yo-yo, but thanks to his ingenuity, it became the favorite toy of millions of people everywhere. Pedro not only made a better life for himself, but he enriched the lives of countless others, adapting a Filipino pastime to create a toy with no limit beyond your imagination.

AUTHOR'S NOTE

I was originally inspired to write this book when I learned that the ever-popular yo-yo toy was credited to a Filipino. Like many historical figures, Pedro did not leave behind an extensive written record of his life, and there was a great deal of missing and conflicting information—even in the Smithsonian National Museum of American History, which holds the archives of the Duncan Toys Company. Eventually, however, author and yo-yo expert Jonathan Auxier put me in touch with Kevin Walters, Pedro's grandson, who shared his memories of his grandfather, as well as his journal. The facts surrounding the life of Pedro Flores and his creation of the yo-yo presented in this book were largely based on those hours of interviews with Kevin, and I thank him for his help and participation.

THE PHILIPPINES

The Philippines is a nation that today consists of more than 7,000 islands in the western Pacific, occupied by 109 million people. A loose group of tribes lived among the Philippine islands when explorer Ferdinand Magellan arrived in 1521. Magellan claimed the islands for Spain, and subsequent Spanish colonizers brought the Catholic religion and other European customs to the Filipinos. Spain ruled the Philippines for more than three hundred years, until 1898, when the United States purchased the islands from Spain.

Filipinos who had rebelled against Spain felt betrayed and continued their fight in a war lasting years. Because the United States had also fought for independence, opinion was divided on taking another people's freedom away. After much debate, the government promised to give Filipinos their freedom back. The Second World War interrupted this process, but the United States kept its word, and after nearly fifty years under American rule, the Philippines became an independent country in 1946.

THE YO-YO

The toy we now know as the yo-yo originated in China thousands of years ago. Then called the bandalore, it traveled west over the centuries to Europe, where it was considered an amusement for adults and the upper class. It appeared in the United States in the mid-nineteenth century but failed to achieve widespread acceptance. The bandalore also spread throughout Asia and the Philippines, where it became highly popular by the late nineteenth century, when Pedro Flores was born. The first printed reference to the term "yo-yo" in the West was in *Scientific American* magazine, which published an article on "Filipino Toys" in a July 1916 issue.

⚘ PEDRO FLORES ⚘

Pedro Edralin Flores was born in Vintar, in the Ilocos Norte province of the Philippines, on April 26, 1896. Not much is known of his early life. When Pedro came to the United States in 1915, it was common for young men to leave their countries and go abroad in search of work—usually difficult, low-paying manual labor in fields or factories. Fewer than 20 percent of all Americans finished high school during this time, but Pedro attended the High School of Commerce in San Francisco (1919–20) and later the University of California at Berkeley and Hastings College of Law in San Francisco.

Although he did not finish college, Pedro started his Yo-Yo Manufacturing Company in Santa Barbara, California, in 1928. His slip-string—a twisted string wrapped loosely around the axle—was a major innovation in yo-yo production, allowing the toy greater flexibility and the ability to "sleep" at the end of the string. Pedro adopted marketing strategies, such as interactive demonstrations and contests, which propelled his toy to national success.

Pedro at first made the yo-yos by hand, selling them for a dime each. Applying what he may have learned in law school, Pedro filed a trademark to protect his rights to the name of the yo-yo in 1930. That same year, two investors, James Lewis and Daniel Stone, gave him money to expand, establishing the Flores and Stone Company in Los Angeles and the Flores Yo-Yo Corporation in Hollywood.

About this time, the Yo-Yo Manufacturing Company relocated to Los Angeles. At this point, machines cut the yo-yos from wood, with factories producing up to tens of thousands of yo-yos per day. A few years later, entrepreneur Donald Duncan bought Pedro's company, including the trademark, and asked Pedro to stay on as his promoter and manage a team of mostly Filipino demonstrators.

During the Great Depression, many businesses shut down and work became scarce. Some people blamed foreigners for taking their jobs away, and riots against Filipino workers forced many to flee back to the Philippines. Pedro continued to promote the yo-yo for the Duncan company around the United States, traveling with his wife—a white woman named Edria—along with other kabayan such as Fred Mendoza, Perfecto Valdez, Joe Radovan, and Fortunato

Anunciacion. The toy remained popular throughout the Great Depression, for it was easy to learn, highly portable, and provided a lot of fun for little cost—as low as 15 cents.

Pedro continued to be involved with yo-yos the rest of his life. In the 1930s, he started the Bandalore Yo-Yo Company in Rockford, Illinois, selling yo-yos with the thin-line design of those he made earlier. Shortly after the outbreak of World War II, Pedro and his family moved to Coshocton, Ohio, his wife's home state, where they lived for more than twenty years until his death in 1963.

BIBLIOGRAPHY

Books

Cassidy, John. *The Klutz Yo-Yo Book*. Klutz Press, 1987.

Hirahara, Noomi. *Distinguished Asian American Business Leader*s. Greenwood Publishing, 2003.

Malko, George. *The One and Only Yo-Yo Book*. Avon Books, 1978.

Zeiger, Helane. *World on a String*. TK Yo-Yos, Ltd., 1989.

Periodicals

Branc, Alva R., Acting Div. Supt. Pampanga. "Filipino Toys. How Our Young Island Wards Amuse Themselves." *Scientific American Supplement No. 2113*, July 1, 1916.

Crosby, David F. "The Yo-Yo: Its Rise and Fall." *American History*, August 2002, pages 53–56.

Crump, Stuart, ed. "Collector's Showcase," *Yo-Yo Times*. Creative Communications, Inc. July 1990, volume 10, No. 5.

Kowalick, Vince. "Yo-Yo Entrepreneur Had to Pull Some Strings." *Los Angeles Times*, May 23, 1994, page 5.

"Pedro Flores: The Filipino Yo-Yo Manufacturer." *Philippine-American Reporter*, November 16, 1929.

"Press-Gazette to Give $75 In Prizes to 'Yo-Yo' Artists; Tournament Being Planned." *Green Bay Press Gazette*, n.d.

"Press To Offer $50 In Prizes For Yo-Yo." *The Sheboygan Press*, May 23, 1933, pages 1 and 16.

"Thank you, Pedro Flores, for the Good Times." *The Palm Beach Post*, May 7, 1973, page 25.

Additional Sources

"The American Yo-Yo Association Home Page."
https://yo-yos.net/american-yo-yo-association/

"Inventor of Flores Yo-Yo: A Philippine Immigrant Defying Odds in the Great Depression."
http://ucifilam.blogspot.com/2009/11/inventor-of-flores-yo-yo-philippine.html

"Yo-Yo." Games and Hobbies. 1998. Retrieved July 02, 2014, from Encyclopedia.com:
http://www.encyclopedia.com/doc/1G2-2896700109.html

Flores, Pedro. "Travel Journal, handwritten," n.d.

Walters, Kevin. Grandson of Pedro Flores. Phone interview by Rob Peñas, May 13, 2022.

The facts in the text were accurate and all hyperlinks were live at the time of the book's original publication. The author and publisher do not assume any responsibility for changes made since that time.